Steven the Snail

Steven the **sn**ail had a **sp**ecial birthday today.

He was turning 5 years old.

Steven's **sp**ecial party was going to be at the old **sp**otty **st**one.

So **St**even **sl**owly **sl**id over a **sp**ikey leaf ...

... **Sl**id under a brown **st**ool ...

... **Sl**id **sl**owly through a spring ...

... **Sl**id over a **sn**ow coloured **sp**oon ...

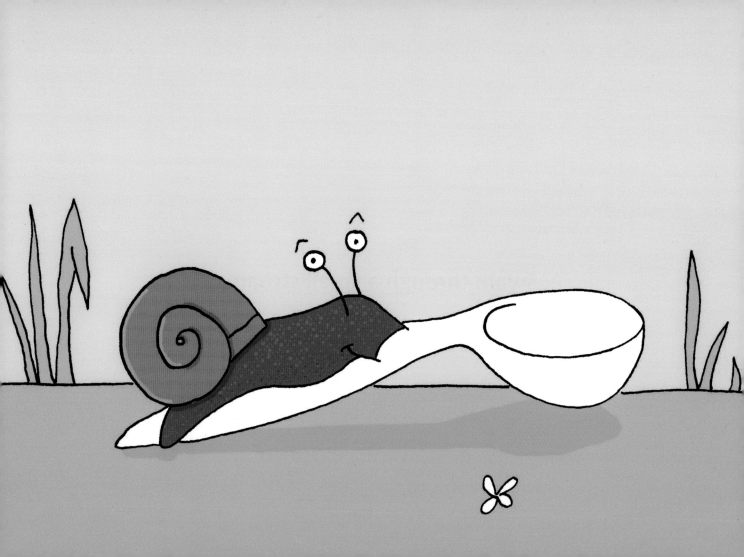

... **Sw**am through a **sm**all stream ...

... **<u>Sl</u>**owly past a **<u>sl</u>**eeping **<u>sp</u>**ider ...

... **<u>Sn</u>**eaked past a **<u>sl</u>**eeping **<u>sn</u>**ake ...

... Just in time for his birthday bash
at the old **sp**otty **st**one.

All **St**even's **sn**ail friends were there to celebrate
his **sp**ecial day. Hurray!